Report

Ashes to Ashes
Beliefs, Trends, and Practices in Dying, Death, and the Afterlife

Marianne Rozario and Lia Shimada
with contribution from Wendy Appenteng Daniels
and Simon Perfect
Foreword by Edward Stourton

Acknowledgements

We would like to thank all who have supported this project. Wendy Appenteng Daniels and Simon Perfect deserve particular mention. For their contributions to the literature reviews, their research on polling data, and above all for the many interviews they conducted, we are deeply grateful.

Our thanks must also be extended to Theos colleagues who have contributed substantially to this project through its various stages. Thanks, in particular, to Paul Bickley for his guidance and wisdom. Chine McDonald, Nick Spencer, Madeleine Pennington, Nathan Mladin, Hannah Rich, and Andrew Graystone deserve our gratitude for reviewing drafts and providing excellent, thought-provoking suggestions. We are also grateful to the Susanna Wesley Foundation, particularly our colleagues Sue Miller and Emma Pavey. This report is richer for their reflections.

Finally, this report would not be possible without the participation of those we interviewed – academics, faith leaders and representatives, death industry professionals, charity leaders, health professionals, community organisers, and the "death-curious". For your time, your passion, your honesty, and for all you brought to this conversation: *thank you.*

Marianne Rozario and Lia Shimada
March 2023

This report in
60 seconds

Theos, in partnership with the Susanna Wesley Foundation, investigated current trends on, and attitudes towards, dying, death, and the afterlife in the UK, and explored the role of churches and faith communities. Our report draws on data from a wide range of experts and informed participants – academics, faith leaders and representatives, death industry professionals, charity leaders, health professionals, and community organisers. We interviewed 33 individuals and 31 focus group participants between June and November 2022.

Our research focused on understanding attitudes surrounding a "good death", trends and practices on memorialisation of the dead, and beliefs about the afterlife. We sought to explore the role played by churches and faith communities offering pastoral care and theological accompaniment.

Common trends to what makes a "good death" include no pain/suffering, being surrounded by family/at home, peace/reconciliation, and preparedness. There is a growing trend to choose cremation over burial, and towards alternative memorialisation practices, with an increased emphasis on "celebrations of life". There exists a wide range of religious and spiritual beliefs about the afterlife, among the religious and the non-religious.

Churches and faith communities walk alongside the dying, offering a voice of reassurance, comfort, and informal support, while spiritually supporting the dying through prayer. They have an important role to play, in offering both pastoral care and theological accompaniment to the dying and the bereaved, but could also expand this role – especially through facilitating increased conversation about, and education on, dying, death, and the afterlife, and equipping their leaders and representatives to develop better pastoral and theological practice.

We close by offering a limited series of recommendtions for death industry professionals, and for churches and faith communities, to refine their delivery of this crucial role.

Foreword

We recently said goodbye to a defiantly atheist neighbour – a distinguished figure in the arts world – at a joyful ceremony in our parish church. The vicar takes the view that the Church of England is for everyone, not just believers, and her fine old church proved wonderfully welcoming to his family, friends and fans.

When my father died eighteen months ago, we buried him at a tiny Catholic chapel he loved, by the banks of a river in the North Yorkshire dales. The Requiem Mass, with its unwavering confidence in resurrection, carried along even those members of his family who have no faith.

Religion – and I am sure this applies just as fully to the United Kingdom's minority faiths as it does to Christianity – still seems to be a source of strength we turn to when confronted with the enormous enigma of death.

And, as this report reflects, death is a subject we were forced to confront on a grand scale during the Covid pandemic. Those grim tallies of Covid deaths read out each afternoon at the official briefings took us back to an earlier era when death was a routine part of life. Because we spent so much time confined to our homes, most of us heard them being repeated on the evening news, so they became part of a communal experience.

Presenting the BBC's *Sunday* programme during those months, I was struck again and again by the tragedy of the lonely goodbyes imposed by lockdown regulations. The pandemic was a powerful lesson in how much a good death – or at least a decent and dignified farewell - matters to those left behind.

As someone with a slow-moving but incurable cancer, I welcome the greater openness about death this report identifies. It is certainly true, as the report finds, that many people are turning to new and more secular ways of celebrating the memory of those they loved, but most religious traditions can call on the experience of centuries of responding to the reality of death, and they have much to offer in a debate of the kind *Ashes to Ashes* seeks to encourage.

Edward Stourton
March 2023

Edward Stourton has worked in broadcasting for over forty years, and regularly presents programmes such as The World at One, The World this Weekend, Sunday and Analysis. He has been a foreign correspondent for Channel 4, ITN, and the BBC, and for ten years he was one of the main presenters of the Today programme. He has published 12 books.

Contents

Executive summary

Theos, in partnership with the Susanna Wesley Foundation, investigated current trends on, and attitudes towards, dying, death, and the afterlife in the UK, and explored the role of churches and faith communities. Our report draws on data from a wide range of experts and informed participants – academics, faith leaders and representatives, death industry professionals, charity leaders, health professionals, and community organisers. Between June and November 2022, we interviewed 33 individuals and 31 focus group participants.

Our research questions inquired: **What are the current trends on, and attitudes towards, dying, death, and the afterlife in the UK? And what role do churches and faith communities play?** Acknowledging current trends, we explored the question: **to what extent do churches and faith communities care for pastorally, and accompany theologically, the dying and the bereaved?**

Our research focuses on understanding attitudes surrounding a "good death", trends and practices on memorialisation of the dead, and beliefs about the afterlife. We found that the common trends to what makes a "good death" include no pain/suffering, being surrounded by family/at home, peace/reconciliation, and preparedness. Our study suggests that there is a growing trend to choose cremation, partly due to costs, but that burials remain popular. The scattering or storing of cremated remains is also a growing practice.

Similarly, there is a trend towards alternative memorialisation practices; funerals are giving way to "celebrations of life" that may incorporate broader "spiritual spectrum". According to our findings, there exists a wide range of religious and spiritual beliefs about the afterlife. While established religions have an understanding of the afterlife and the concept of the soul, among faith leaders and believers this understanding is often diverse and amorphous.

We sought to explore the role played by churches and faith communities, in relation to the themes of dying, death, and the afterlife. Our research found that they walk alongside the dying, offering a voice of reassurance, comfort, and informal support, while spiritually supporting the dying through prayer. Our study also highlighted the importance of ritual frameworks for farewell; in particular, religious funerals offered by churches and faith communities create space in which people can grapple with the nuanced emotional complexities of death. Furthermore, the idea of an afterlife comforted the dying and the bereaved by offering a spiritual framework for navigating life and death.

We suggest that **churches and faith communities have an important role to play, in offering both pastoral care and theological accompaniment to the dying and the bereaved.** We define "pastoral care" as a framework of emotional, social, and – crucially – spiritual support to those facing death and to the bereaved. We define "theological accompaniment" as a framework of walking alongside the dying and bereaved, through offering space and opportunity to explore distinctly religious understandings of living in the context of dying, death, and afterlife.

Pastorally, churches and faith communities support and care for us when death approaches. Theologically, churches and faith communities help us prepare for death by encouraging wider conversation about the meaning of life and death, helping people explore themes of hope, and the continued existence after physical death. Churches and faith communities could improve their practice through facilitating increased conversation about, and education on, dying, death, and the afterlife, and equipping their leaders and representatives to develop better pastoral and theological practice.

Introduction

Death may have a rising profile in public conversation, yet on a personal level, we tend towards avoidance.

We have seen an upsurge of discussion on the topic of death in the media and in popular culture. Dame Deborah James, co-founder of the podcast *You, Me and the Big C*, rose to fame through discussing her cancer illness. The podcast reached number one in the UK podcast charts and was noted for its light-hearted approach to the topic. Similarly, Kathryn Mannix's book *With the End in Mind*, which explores end-of-life stories from her time working in palliative care medicine, was a *Sunday Times* bestseller following its publication in 2019. The book has widely been recognised as imparting wisdom on how to live and die well.

The COVID-19 pandemic brought the subject of death acutely into the public realm while bridging the personal boundary – through broadcasts of daily death tolls, lockdown funerals, and the inability to have common practices and rituals in both end-of-life circumstances and post-death. Understanding attitudes to death has now become marked by pre-COVID-19 or post-COVID-19 language.

Deaths of prominent people, furthermore, keep the topic in society's public consciousness. In 2022, we saw the deaths of Her Majesty Queen Elizabeth II, the footballer Pelé, and Pope Benedict XVI, among others. Their deaths were the centre of news broadcasts and attracted outpourings of public grief in the UK and internationally.

Despite the upsurge of death in public conversations and in popular culture, most of us do not think too deeply about the uncomfortable reality of our own mortality or of those we love. This inability to talk about our own death results in us being unprepared for it. In 2015, it was reported that just 36% of

Britons had written a will, and only 21% had talked about their own death with someone else.[1] Perhaps there has been a slight improvement in recent years – in part due to an increase in public conversations on death and in part due to the impact of COVID-19. During the first lockdown, many legal practitioners reported a high volume of enquiries relating to will planning, yet a recent study assessing post-pandemic attitudes revealed that 44% of its respondents had not discussed financial arrangements in the event of their death.[2] Evidently, there is still a long way to go to become a society that fosters open and honest conversations about dying, death, and the afterlife.

Furthermore, when death is noted in the public sphere, it is normally through statistics or tragic personal stories, rather than as a catalyst for spiritual or religious reflection. Even though traditionally churches and faith communities have been the custodians of death in the UK, religious dimensions on these topics often go amiss.

Emerging from this ambiguous backdrop, our research asks the following questions: **What are the current trends on, and attitudes towards, dying, death, and the afterlife in the UK? And what role do churches and faith communities play? To what extent do churches and faith communities care for pastorally, and accompany theologically, the dying and the bereaved?**

Purpose of the study

Our research was a partnership between Theos and the Susanna Wesley Foundation. The purpose of our study was to investigate current trends on, and attitudes towards, dying, death, and the afterlife in the UK, with an analytical focus on the role of churches and faith communities. We interviewed a wide range of experts and informed participants – religious and non-religious – to gather perspectives on current trends in the UK. Using existing polling data and published literature, as well as our original qualitative data, our report informs and describes current attitudes towards the concept of a "good death", trends and practices on memorialisation of the dead, and beliefs about the afterlife. Intertwined with these themes, our report explores the role of churches and faith communities through pastoral care and theological accompaniment.

Methodology

Our report is informed by mixed-methods qualitative research. In total, we conducted in-depth interviews with 64 participants from across England, Scotland, Wales, and Northern Ireland, roughly half of whom were individual interviewees and the other half were focus group participants.

Between June and November 2022, we conducted a series of 33 semi-structured individual interviews. The interviewees were selected because they were experts or informed individuals fitting into one or more of the following categories: academics, faith leaders and representatives, death industry professionals, charity leaders, health professionals, and community organisers. Out of those individually interviewed, 18 were Christian, two were Muslim, and two were of other faiths: Jewish and Buddhist. A further three were non-religious, identifying as agnostic, humanist, and atheist. The faith identities of the remaining eight remain unknown. Over half of the individual interviewees were Christian, representing a range of denominations including Anglican, Catholic, Methodist, and Baptist.

In addition to the individual interviews, six focus groups with 31 participants in total were held between June and November 2022: two interfaith groups, two Death Café groups, a young-person, and an elderly person focus group. We choose these groups to represent a large demographic of age, and religious and non-religious beliefs. The interfaith focus groups had ten participants representing faith leaders, faith community organisers, and academics: four Christians, two Muslims, two Jewish, a Hindu, and a Sikh participant. The nine Death Café participants were recruited based on their familiarity with the subject of death, irrespective of religious affiliation. The young-person focus group drew on five tertiary education students from a London university. Although participants were religiously diverse (Buddhist, Christian, and Muslim), they were not selected for their religious background. In order to capture a cross-generational conversation, the final focus group consisted of seven elderly people associated with a Christian community group.

Structure of the report

The report is divided into five chapters. The **context** chapter presents a brief historical contextualisation of the invisibility of death in Britain, the Death Positivity movement and rise of Death Cafés, as well as the conversational shift caused by COVID-19. The next three chapters describe attitudes towards and trends on dying, death, and the afterlife in the UK, using both existing polling data and data from our qualitative interviews. The **dying** chapter describes current attitudes to the question of "what makes a good death?" through highlighting four recurring themes from our data: no suffering or pain; dying at home surrounded by loved ones; peace and reconciliation; and preparedness. The **death** chapter identifies trends and practices related to the body post-death and to memorialisation of the dead. The **afterlife** chapter outlines attitudes to concepts of the afterlife through both religious and non-religious frameworks, as well as diverse concepts of the soul. In our **final chapter**, we synthesise our faith-specific analyses to explore the role churches and faith communities play through pastoral care and theological accompaniment. The report concludes with some guided recommendations targeted at churches and faith communities, and death industry professionals.

1 Aaron O'Neill, *"Life expectancy (from birth) in the United Kingdom from 1765 to 2020"*, Statista, 21 June 2022, www.statista.com/statistics/1040159/lifeexpectancy-united-kingdom-all-time

2 Matthew Duncan, "It's good to talk: financial planning and wills", *Solicitors Journal* 164 (2021), p. 56.

1 Context

(In)visibility of death

Before the advent of modernity, death was the order of the day. Driven by high rates of infant mortality and the rapid spread of lethal, infectious disease, death was a regular presence in everyday life. Life expectancy (from birth) was 40.53 years in 1820, and 48.89 years in 1920, compared with 81.15 years in 2020.[1] People tended to die at home, cared for by their family and community.[2]

With advances in medicine, death became increasingly peripheral, confined within institutions like hospitals and care homes.[3] The process of dying was increasingly professionalised. Pre-COVID-19, the percentage of deaths at a hospital for all ages in England alone was 44% as opposed to only 28% dying at home. Funeral directors tend to have sole responsibility for the removal of the body post-death – thus further curtailing societal familiarity with death. We now tend to view death through the lens of life-extending medicine, therefore seeing death itself as a medical failure.

Life expectancy (from birth) was 40.53 years in 1820, and 48.89 years in 1920, compared with 81.15 years in 2020. With advances in medicine, death became increasingly peripheral, confined within institutions like hospitals and care homes.

Not surprisingly, the British public has an uncomfortable relationship with death. Over a decade ago, research commissioned by the Dying Matters coalition found that two-thirds of Britons feel uncomfortable when discussing death and dying.[4] Recent data from a 2021 survey suggest minimal change. Although 84% of Britons say that there is nothing preventing them from talking about death, only 14% have actively engaged with the subject and expressed their end-of-life preferences and wishes.[5] This gap reveals a dissonance between what people believe and what people do: it is symptomatic of a society that keeps death "crushed under the heel of avoidance and deferral".[6]

The phenomenon of "death discomfort" was apparent in our study. Interviewees expressed frustration with "dreadful euphemisms", "lack of compassionate language" (particularly in the medical sector and the funeral industry), and the "enormous stigma" of a "taboo and sensitive" subject. In the words of one exasperated priest: "If you won't say the word 'dying', how are you going to manage it?" Throughout this study, interviewees recounted a range of challenging implications. For example, an inability to talk honestly and coherently about death can lead to negative effects on mental health and wellbeing, as well as entrenched intergenerational conflict. One Sikh scholar described tensions she has observed within families, driven by the reluctance of older members to write wills or discuss their end-of-life wishes; these dynamics are by no means confined to Sikh communities. Reluctance to engage in discussion can also have far-reaching relational impact, leading people to avoid those who are bereaved – thus fuelling and perpetuating the cycle of "death discomfort" in our society.

66

In the words of one exasperated priest: "If you won't say the word 'dying', how are you going to manage it?"

"Death discomfort" can have profound implications for bereavement. The difficulties that people report in discussing death and dying can leave them ill-equipped to support those who are grieving, with 28% of respondents to a 2020 poll admitting that they would feel uncomfortable speaking to a recently bereaved individual.[7] People tend to worry about saying the wrong thing – though in fact, most of us report that if we were bereaved, we would prefer that someone say the wrong thing than say nothing at all.[8] Sadly, in a poll from 2020, over a tenth (11%) of people bereaved in the previous five years reported that "no one did anything" to support or comfort them.[9]

Yet there are hopeful signs that the British public may be developing an appetite for conversation. In a 2018 poll, a third of respondents indicated that they thought about death at least once per week.[10] When it comes to death talk, there is growing evidence that society is improving gradually.[11] Momentum appears to be gathering pace; there are signs that discussions of death are increasingly normalised, thus giving death the visibility it deserves.

There are signs that discussions of death are increasingly normalised.

Towards "death positivity"?

In 2011, the American mortician and writer Caitlin Doughty founded The Order of the Good Death – a community of funeral industry professionals, academics, and artists who explore ways to reframe end-of-life possibilities.[12] Through her extensive advocacy work and media outreach, Doughty has become the figurehead of the emerging "Death Positive Movement"[13] based on the conviction that "honest conversations about death and dying [are] the cornerstone of a healthy society".[14] Although the campaigning efforts of The Order of the Good Death remain largely focused on the US, its "death-positive" message has international implications.

Presently, Death Cafés can be viewed as a grassroots movement in and of themselves, or an archetypal example of what the "Death Positive Movement" has led to. Death Cafés are a "pop-up" network of groups open to people from all backgrounds who gather in an informal setting to talk about death. The objective is to "increase awareness of death with a view to helping people make the most of their (finite) lives." Death Cafés avowedly are neither bereavement support nor grief counselling sites, but rather, as sociologist Jack Fong points out, encounters with mortality in ways that are life-affirming. The concept originated from "cafés mortels" coined by Bernard Crettaz, a Swiss writer and ethnologist, around 2004. Subsequently, Jon Underwood, a Buddhist London-based business developer, imported the concept to the UK, with the first UK-based Death Café taking place in Hackney in September 2011.[16] The Baby Boomer generation (born 1946-1964) is the primary age group represented in Death Cafés.[17] Globally, over 7,500 Death Cafés are held across 63 countries, with nearly 3,000 in the UK alone.[18]

New narratives: impact and opportunities from COVID-19

COVID-19 has changed the track of conversations around death. During the pandemic, the subject of death dominated the media landscape; it shifted from being a peripheral topic to receiving a "political reply".[19] Through daily media coverage of the national death toll, death was re-integrated into everyday life and made visible again. By mid-2020, there was an increase of deaths in a usual year by 67%, which amounted to a total of 55,000

66

During the pandemic, the subject of death shifted from being a peripheral topic to receiving a "political reply".

additional deaths. In addition, an estimated 9.7 million people
have been unable to attend funerals for their loved ones during
lockdown restrictions in the UK.[20]

Not surprisingly, the pandemic weighed heavily on those
we interviewed for our research. Many participants were eager
to discuss the losses they witnessed, and to reflect on longer-
term implications for their life and work. The chaplaincy
director of a large, national network of care homes described
particularly traumatic loss, with around 50% of residents dying
due to COVID-19 in a short space of time. Several interviewees
observed ongoing stigma around deaths from COVID-19,
with people reluctant to admit the cause and, by extension,
unable to seek the pastoral care they might need. Above all,
interviewees cited the painful loss of ritual frameworks around
death.

Across the spectrum, the pandemic re-shaped our
experiences and practices of grief. "People felt cheated in
the pandemic," remarked one participant of an interfaith
focus group. She described times when her Orthodox Jewish
community struggled to form a *minyan* (the minimum number
of people required for communal prayer). In addition, "because
you couldn't gather, you couldn't have the proper *shiva*"
(formal mourning period). Another faith leader described
the death, during the first lockdown, of a key figure in his
dispersed Christian community. The community experienced
"muted, limited processing of grief in terms of liturgy, in terms
of public or shared grieving." The "strangeness of grief" was
exacerbated by the prolonged, exhausting period between
the death of a loved one and their public memorial service –
an experience shared by countless grieving individuals and
communities.

Yet the pandemic has also created new opportunities for increased engagement with death. "People have had to confront their own mortality. The pandemic brought things into sharp focus," observed an end-of-life doula. She cited an increase in the number of conversations she now has with people who wish to make advanced plans. End-of-life doulas are non-medical professionals "trained to care for a terminally ill person's physical, emotional, and spiritual needs during the death process."[21] Along similar lines, several chaplains interviewed for this study reported having "more human and more meaningful conversations" as society has moved through and out of the pandemic.

Faith communities, like the rest of society, have learned to respond flexibly during the pandemic. According to one imam based in Glasgow: "Religion had to adapt, to facilitate ways of making it easier for people and being sensitive to their needs." He described how scholars of Islam addressed the prohibition on the numbers of mourners by exploring "flexibilities" for reciting funeral prayers in alternative locations. Another Muslim faith leader recalled how mosques, which previously would not have worked together, intentionally chose to work together during COVID-19. A Jewish chaplain spoke of positive interfaith encounters – for example, a conversation with a Muslim family as they waited outside a hospital where their mother had died; he spoke with them about the significance of her dying on a holy day. Across the religious spectrum, faith leaders have adopted, and sometimes embraced, the now-common practice of streaming funerals and memorial services online. In this way, the pandemic widened participation in memorial activities, facilitating larger numbers of people to engage with death.

According to a YouGov study in 2021, a quarter of UK adults (25%) say that the pandemic has affected their views on death, and three-quarters of this group reported becoming more worried about losing a loved one.[22] The study also recorded that 46% stated that they

A quarter of UK adults (25%) say that the pandemic has affected their views on death.

were thinking about death more than they did pre-COVID-19.[23] A separate study found that nearly a quarter (24%) of adults in the UK say the pandemic has made them more likely to have informal conversations about their death.[24] This is a significant shift from the pre-COVID-19 situation – *fewer* people see our society as uncomfortable with death talk.

COVID-19 has generated different levels of expectation on how death discourse will develop. On the one hand, COVID-19 has afforded society the insight of incorporating and rethinking the significance of death. On the other hand, major work needs to be done to unpack a "shadow pandemic of dysfunctional grief".[25] While death tolls were being acknowledged, funeral lockdowns, the normalisation of virtual goodbyes, and oversight of non-COVID-19 related deaths all contributed to creating a parallel "grief pandemic" of people processing grief in atypical circumstances.

Trends: dying, death, and the afterlife

Our research investigated and examined current trends on, and attitudes towards, dying, death, and the afterlife in the UK, through analysing existing polling data and through interviewing a wide range of experts and informed participants. We interviewed a wide selection of academics, faith leaders and representatives, death industry professionals, charity leaders, health professionals, and community organisers, as well as orchestrated targeted focus groups representing informed participants from a spectrum of ages and religious beliefs. All interviews were conducted between June and November 2022.

The next three chapters inform and describe current attitudes surrounding a "good death"; trends and practices related to the body post-death and memorialisation of the dead; and beliefs about the afterlife.

1 Aaron O'Neill, "Life expectancy (from birth) in the United Kingdom from 1765 to 2020", *Statista*, 21 June 2022, www.statista.com/statistics/1040159/ lifeexpectancy-united-kingdom-all-time

2 Panagiotis Pentaris and Kate Woodthorpe, "Familiarity with death" in Panagiotis Pentaris (ed), *Death, Grief and Loss in the Context of COVID-19* (Abingdon, Oxon: Routledge, 2021), p. 26.

3 "End of life care profiles", *Public Health England*, 6 February 2018, www.gov.uk/ government/publications/end-of-life-care-profiles-february-2018-update/ statistical-commentary-end-of-life-care-profiles-february-2018-update

4 "Dying Matters Death and Dying Survey", Savanta, 15 May 2011, www.savanta. com/knowledge-centre/poll/dying-matters-death-and-dying-survey-3/

5 A Nelson et al., "Public attitudes to death and dying in the UK" (Marie Curie, 2021).

6 Yasmin Gunaratnam, "Death matters: so why do the British hate talking about it?", *Goldsmiths University of London*, 6 June 2015, www.gold.ac.uk/news/ comment-death-matters/

7 "Hospice UK Dying Matters Awareness Week Polling", *Savanta*, 11 May 2020, www.savanta.com/knowledge-centre/poll/ hospice-uk-dying-matters-awareness-week-polling/

8 In a 2020 poll, 71% of Britons said they would prefer someone accidentally to say the wrong thing to them if they were recently bereaved than to say nothing at all. "Hospice UK Dying Matters Awareness Week Polling", *Savanta*, 11 May 2020, www.savanta.com/knowledge-centre/poll/hospice-uk-dying- matters-awareness-week-polling/, p. 36. Great Britain only.

9 "Hospice UK Dying Matters Awareness Week Polling", *Savanta*, 11 May 2020, www.savanta.com/knowledge-centre/poll/hospice-uk-dying-matters- awareness-week-polling/, p. 51. Great Britain only.

10 "Hospice UK / NCPC: Dying Matters Survey 2018", *Savanta*, 14 May 2018, www.savanta.com/knowledge-centre/poll/hospice-uk-ncpc-dying-matters- survey-2018/, p. 24.

11 "Dying Matters Coalition – Public opinion on death and dying", *Savanta*, 12 May 2016, www.savanta.com/knowledge-centre/poll/dying-matters-coalition- public-opinion-on-death-and-dying/, p. 15. Great Britain only; "Hospice UK Dying Matters Awareness Week Polling", *Savanta*, 11 May 2020, www.savanta. com/knowledge-centre/poll/hospice-uk-dying-matters-awareness-week- polling/, pp. 4-5. Great Britain only.

12 www.orderofthegooddeath.com/

13 Kim Kelly, "Welcome the reaper: Caitlin Doughty and the 'death-positivity' Movement", *The Guardian*, 27 October 2017, www.theguardian.com/books/2017/oct/27/caitlin-doughty-death-positivity

14 www.orderofthegooddeath.com/death-positive-movement/

15 Jack Fong, *The Death Café Movement: Exploring the Horizons of Mortality* (Cham, Switzerland: Springer International Publishing, 2017).

16 Iliana Magra, "Jon Underwood, Founder of Death Café Movement, Dies at 44", *The New York Times*, 12 July 2017, www.nytimes.com/2017/07/11/international-home/jon-underwood-dead-death-cafe-movement

17 Jack Fong, "Baby Boomers and the Death Café" in *The Death Café Movement.*

18 "Dying Well", Global Wellness Summit, www.globalwellnesssummit.com/2019-global-wellness-trends/dying-well/ www.deathcafe.com

19 Panagiotis Pentaris and Kate Woodthorpe, "Familiarity with death" in *Death, Grief and Loss in the Context of COVID-19*, p. 27.

20 "A nation in mourning", *Co-op Funeralcare Media Report*, July 2020, www.coop.co.uk/funeralcare/nationinmourning

21 "How 'Death Doulas' Can Help People at the End of Their Life", *Healthline*, 15 July 2018, www.healthline.com/health-news/how-death-doulas-can-help-people-at-the-end-of-their-life

22 "The YouGov Death Study", *YouGov*, 6 October 2021, www.yougov.co.uk/topics/society/articles-reports/2021/10/06/yougov-death-study

23 Ibid.

24 "Public attitudes, cultural perspectives and engagement", *Hospice UK*, 2022, p. 5. UK-wide. https://hukstage-bucket.s3.eu-west-2.amazonaws.com/s3fs-public/2022-01/Hospice%20UK%20submission%20to%20UK%20Commission%20on%20Bereavement.pdf, p. 5. UK-wide.

25 Lauren Breen et al., "Grief and functional impairment following COVID-19 loss in a treatment-seeking sample: the mediating role of meaning", *British Journal of Guidance & Counselling* (2022), pp. 1-12.

2   Dying

We interviewed a wide selection of experts and informed individuals to understand trends in the UK on what people want as they are dying. Principally, we asked the interviewees "what makes a 'good death'?". This chapter explains the answer to that question through analysing existing polling data and our interview data.

2.1 Polling analysis

What makes a "good death"?

While there is no univocal consensus on what constitutes a "good death", there are recurring examples given to describe one. According to polling data, for most British people a "good death" is one which is pain-free, surrounded by loved ones, and maintains the dying person's dignity. These factors appear top in three polls each held in the years between 2014 and 2016.[1] By some margin, painlessness is the most desired factor – in each poll, 50-52% of the population ranked being pain-free as the most (or second-most) important thing for them when imagining a "good death".[2] The vast majority of us fear dying in pain even more than we fear dying alone, or a close relative or friend dying. A 2011 poll found that 83% of people agree that they are scared of dying in pain (54% very scared), compared to 62% who say they are scared of dying alone, and 77% scared of a close friend or family member dying.[3]

Being with family and friends, and retaining dignity, are the most/second-most important considerations for about a third of people (35%).[4] For a fifth, it is being involved in decisions about one's care/family being involved, or being cared for and dying in a place you choose.[5] Less than 10% prioritise having religious or spiritual needs met – and in fact, nearly two-thirds of people ranked this factor as the least important out of the available options.[6]

According to polling data, the COVID-19 pandemic does not appear to have caused a big shift in what we want in a "good death". A UK-wide poll in 2021 found that people's top three priorities for their final days of life are being free of pain (47%), being surrounded by loved ones (43%), and being able to maintain dignity and self-respect (35%).[7]

How prepared are we when it comes to death?

Another important aspect of a "good death" is end-of-life preparedness. Looking at multiple Savanta ComRes polls from 2014 to 2019, there appears to be not only a lack of preparedness for death but a trend towards less preparedness. Only just over a third of UK adults (approximately 35%) had written a will.[8] Responding to whether they had informed someone of their funeral wishes, just over a quarter responded positively. Relatively few Britons (around 20%) have discussed their own end-of-life wishes, and marginally fewer have asked a family member about their end-of-life wishes. Even fewer (6%) had written down any wishes or preferences about future care should they not be able to make decisions themselves.[9]

There appears to be not only a lack of preparedness for death but a trend towards less preparedness.

Despite the far greater visibility of death during the pandemic and an increase in informal conversations about it, there is still a big gap between intentions and actions. Significantly, only a tenth of people (10%) who describe themselves as being in the last years of life have made any advance care plans, and a similar amount have made financial

> ❝
> The COVID-19 experience has perhaps made us more comfortable to speak about death, but there are no signs that this has led to action when it comes to end-of-life preparations.

arrangements for their funeral or have a living will.[10] While half of Britons (49%) say that they have pictured their funeral,[11] a study by Co-op Funeralcare in September 2020 estimated that just 9% of those aged 50 and over have a funeral plan in place, and 74% of UK adults say recent events had not encouraged them to discuss their later life wishes with loved ones.[12] The COVID-19 experience has perhaps made us more comfortable to speak about death, but there are no signs that this has led to action when it comes to end-of-life preparations.

2.2 Data analysis

> ❝
> What makes a 'good death'? Four recurring themes appeared: (1) no suffering or pain; (2) dying at home surrounded by loved ones; (3) peace and reconciliation; and (4) preparedness.

Understandings of a "good death"

We explicitly asked our interviewees "what makes a 'good death'". Four recurring themes appeared: (1) no suffering or pain; (2) dying at home surrounded by loved ones; (3) peace and reconciliation; and (4) preparedness. It must also be noted that numerous interviewees expressed that a "good death" could not be generalised but is rather an individual matter.

Definition: a "good death"

The concept of a "good death" is contentious with no agreed definition. Labelling a death as either "good" or "bad" should be met with caution.[13] That holding true, the London End of Life Care Clinical Network associated with the National Health Service defines a "good death" as "the best death that can be achieved in the context of the individual's clinical diagnosis and symptoms, as well as the specific social, cultural and spiritual circumstances, taking into consideration patient and carer wishes and professional expertise."[14] Current literature in sociology uses a list of attributes to characterise a "good death": "being in control, being comfortable, a sense of closure, affirmation/value of the dying person recognised, trust in care providers, recognition of impending death, beliefs and values honoured, burden minimised, relationships optimised, appropriateness of death, leaving a legacy and family care."[15]

The use of the term "good death" had mixed responses by our interviewees. An academic deemed that the term "failed dramatically" to be properly defined and was instead a vague concept which homogenises experiences and contradicts a person-centred care approach. Others drew out scenarios where a "good death" as explained above could not be possible – for example, in the cases of a sudden death or traumatic death, such as a road accident. A charity leader commented that they didn't find the language of a "good death" to be helpful, because "it presupposes that there's a sort of league table, and I've got to the top position, if I've experienced X, Y." Additionally, an academic and Christian faith leader proposed that death could not ever be considered "good" on theological grounds that if life is "good", and if death is the negation of life, then logically, death must be "bad".

(1) No suffering/pain

Numerous interviewees mentioned, in agreement with polling data explored above, that a "good death" is one that either does not involve suffering or dying in pain, or one where pain is minimised. An academic and Christian faith leader stated that, "obviously nobody wants pain when they're dying." Similarly, a charity leader spoke of a "good death" as "a death where there is less (sic) suffering possible".

Healthcare professionals we interviewed spoke of modern medicine, especially palliative care medicine, being able to a greater extent than before get on top of pain management for those dying.

You know, symptoms like pain, we can get on top of them. Modern medicine can sort that out. Breathlessness, we can sort that out as well. All of these symptoms that are sort of distressing for a family to see, most of the time, we have strategies to reduce if not minimise or obliterate it. (Healthcare professional)

Hospices were also highlighted as places for the most effective pain management. An end-of-life doula remarked that despite people's resistance to going into a hospice because it assumes death is close, hospices were amazing resources, able to offer pain alleviation to a dying person.

It was furthermore noted that often the perceived pain of a loved one dying is perhaps different from the reality. For example, laboured breathing at the end of life is often perceived as distress. However, a charity leader spoke of it as "a natural part of the body breaking down and relaxing." Realising this natural process, she suggested, may also give peace to those bereaved who often, without this explanation, hold on to the last memory of their loved one in distress.

(2) At home/surrounded by loved ones

Several interviewees described a "good death" as one whereby the dying person was at home rather than in a hospital environment. An academic and Christian faith leader remarked that "almost everybody wants to die at home". In a personal capacity, a doctor spoke of a "good death" being "probably as not medicalised as possible. And as sort of natural as possible in an environment surrounded by people that I love and care about is probably a 'good death'." The importance of dying surrounded by loved ones was also strongly highlighted by those we interviewed. Charity leaders and death industry professionals all commented that a "good death" would be when your loved ones or very significant people to you are with you by your side.

Conversely, it was also suggested by multiple interviewees that at the moment of death, the dying person might want fewer people present, while others would prefer to die alone:

There is quite good palliative care research data that suggests that people kind of overestimate how much they want people around... sometimes the person dies, like, within minutes of a family leaving the room. (Academic and Christian faith leader)

(3) Peace and reconciliation

A peaceful end to life was also suggested as important. Interviewees suggested that this came about having lived a good life. One academic spoke of a "good death" as one that "comes at the end of a life that you've lived well, whether that be long or short." This idea was reflected by a Muslim faith leader who stated, "So, the idea of death, it is as 'good' as you lived your life, I suppose. So, the idea is that if you've lived a Muslim-conscious life, you will embrace this."

That idea was more profound for those struggling with peace while living:

> *For many people, particularly with serious mental health problems, the way they would describe a 'good death' will be about a search for peace, and the search for a place that is calm, and helps to resolve some of the challenges of their lives.*
> (Charity leader)

A peaceful end also meant, for some Christian participants, having specific religious rituals adhered to.

That peaceful end also meant, for some Christian participants, having specific religious rituals adhered to. One Christian representative of an interfaith group stated, "Oh, for me I think a 'good death' would be: I have sort of cleaned everything up, everything's sorted. So, I've had a confession with the priest." Similarly, an Anglican priest said:

> *Well, I mean, there are the traditional things, which the Church's practice of confession, in a sense, dealt with, which is: Have I put everything right? Am I leaving everything in order?... Should I have made it up with this person? I haven't spoken to my family for the last 20 years. Should I do that?*

(4) Preparedness

Being prepared for death was also highlighted by those interviewed as being conducive to a "good death" – both when death was imminent or simply having "consideration of the fact that you are mortal, and that your life will come to an end at some point". (Charity leader)

Preparedness included having some time to say goodbye to family, friends, and loved ones. An academic and Christian faith leader commented that a sudden death was undesirable, and people more generally wanted some time but not too much time before dying.

> *They need the chance to finish up and tie up loose endings. That makes a real difference to having a good death. I think people feel like they've said the things they need to say. Maybe left letters for people.* (End-of-life doula and funeral celebrant)

By achieving this, it was also found that loved ones were ready to let the dying person go and the dying person was ready to be let go. At that stage, death did not feel sudden or a shock, but had been well prepared.

There is also a desire to have the dying person's affairs in order on a practical level. Multiple interviewees suggested that such practical or logistical matters included ensuring a will was up to date, possessions and financial matters were in hand, and a lasting power of attorney was in place.

There is also a desire to have the dying person's affairs in order on a practical level.

Numerous interviewees from a religious background also spoke of preparedness in terms of the correct logistics surrounding the removal of the body. This was especially the case for Muslim interviewees who spoke of the necessity of upholding Islamic rituals, both immediately after death as well as ensuring correct funeral arrangements. Muslim leaders recalled wishes of the dying person asking the chaplain to ensure that their body was washed and prayed over according to their religious beliefs and rituals. Being entrusted with such requests was considered an honour and privilege by the chaplains. Healthcare professionals were seen to be knowledgeable about these Islamic rituals, but the dying person most often entrusted these requests to the chaplain.

Faith perspective: a "good death"

Faith leaders and representatives we interviewed presented diverse religious beliefs about what makes a "good death". Imams and other Islamic representatives gave examples of a "good death" including dying on a Friday as it is a holy day, dying due to a plague, by drowning, from childbirth, while doing righteous deeds, in a mosque, or while praying, or dying in Mecca or Medina. A Muslim faith leader described that in Islam a "good ending" referred to a person who lives his life in obedience to God, is "adhering to the do's and don'ts of what Islam teaches them." A Hindu academic spoke of an understanding in Hinduism of the need to break the cycle of reincarnation and obtain *moksha* or liberation and be with God, in peace forever. A Christian who works as a celebrant suggested that:

> a "good death" was found in the assurance of being part of the memory of God, joining his kingdom, whatever language you use, this blessing, assurance, that, yes, you're saved, you're redeemed, you've got nothing to fear. And it's just a peaceful exit from this world into glory.

1 These polls covered England, Scotland, and Wales only.

2 "NCPC: Dying Matters Survey", *Savanta*, 11 May 2014, www.savanta.com/
knowledge-centre/poll/ncpc-dying-matters-survey/, pp. 87-101; "National
Council for Palliative Care – Public Opinion on Death and Dying", *Savanta*, 18
May 2015, www.savanta.com/knowledge-centre/poll/ncpc-dying-matters-
survey/, pp. 20-32; "Dying Matters Coalition – Public opinion on death and
dying", *Savanta*, 12 May 2016, www.savanta.com/knowledge-centre/poll/
ncpc-dying-matters-survey/, pp. 38-50. Great Britain only.

3 "Dying Matters Death and Dying Survey", *Savanta*, 15 May 2011, www.savanta.
com/knowledge-centre/poll/dying-matters-death-and-dying-survey-3/, pp.
5-7; "NCPC: Dying Matters Survey", *Savanta*, 11 May 2014, www.savanta.com/
knowledge-centre/poll/ncpc-dying-matters-survey/, p. 1. Great Britain only.

4 "National Council for Palliative Care – Public Opinion on Death and
Dying", *Savanta*, 18 May 2015, www.savanta.com/knowledge-centre/poll/
national-council-for-palliative-care-public-opinion-on-death-and-dying/

5 Ibid.

6 "NCPC: Dying Matters Survey" (2014), www.savanta.com/knowledge-
centre/poll/ncpc-dying-matters-survey/, pp. 87-101; "National Council for
Palliative Care – Public Opinion on Death and Dying" (2015), www.savanta.
com/knowledge-centre/poll/ncpc-dying-matters-survey/, pp. 20-32; "Dying
Matters Coalition – Public opinion on death and dying" (2016), www.savanta.
com/knowledge-centre/poll/ncpc-dying-matters-survey/, pp. 38-50. Great
Britain only.

7 "Public attitudes to death and dying in the UK", *Marie Curie Palliative Care
Research Centre, Division of Population Medicine, Cardiff University School of
Medicine*, https://www.mariecurie.org.uk/globalassets/media/documents/
policy/public-attitudes-to-death-and-dying-report-final.pdf

8 "NCPC: Dying Matters Survey" (2014), www.savanta.com/knowledge-centre/
poll/ncpc-dying-matters-survey/

9 "NCPC: Dying Matters Survey" (2014), www.savanta.com/knowledge-centre/
poll/ncpc-dying-matters-survey/, p. 106; "National Council for Palliative Care
– Public Opinion on Death and Dying" (2015), www.savanta.com/knowledge-
centre/poll/ncpc-dying-matters-survey/, p. 14; "Dying Matters Coalition
– Public opinion on death and dying" (2016), www.savanta.com/knowledge-
centre/poll/ncpc-dying-matters-survey/, p. 29; "Hospice UK / Dying Matters
– Are We Ready April 2019 Survey", *Savanta*, 3 May 2019, www.savanta.com/
knowledge-centre/poll/ncpc-dying-matters-survey/, p. 1. Great Britain only.

10 "Public attitudes to death and dying in the UK", www.mariecurie.org.uk/
globalassets/media/documents/policy/public-attitudes-to-death-and-dying-
report-final.pdf, p. 21.

11 "The YouGov Death Study", *YouGov*, 6 October 2021, www.yougov.co.uk/topics/society/articles-reports/2021/10/06/yougov-death-study

12 "Co-op estimates that 23 million over 50s are unprepared for the inevitable", Co-op, 14 September 2020, www.co-operative.coop/media/news-releases/coop-estimates-that-23-million-over-50s-are-unprepared-for-the-inevitable

13 Karen Steinhauser and James Tulsky, "Defining a 'good' death" in Nathan Cherny (ed) et al., *Oxford Textbook of Palliative Medicine* (Oxford, Oxford University Press: 2015), pp. 77-83.

14 "What is a good death?", *London End of Life Care Clinical Network*, www.england.nhs.uk/london/wp-content/uploads/sites/8/2020/03/WhatIsAGoodDeath.pdf

15 Karen Kehl, "Moving toward peace: an analysis of the concept of a good death", *American Journal of Hospice and Palliative Medicine 23 4 (2006)*, pp. 277-286.

3. Death

Drawing on existing polling data and our interviews with a wide range of experts and informed participants, this chapter identifies and describes trends related to (a) the body post-death and (b) memorialisation of the dead. Specifically, it highlights current practices of burial and cremation, as well as trends associated with funerals and "celebrations of life".

66

As a society, the UK has a high cremation rate. However, people who identify as "practising religious" were more likely to prefer burial to cremation.

3.1 Polling analysis

After a death, the foremost practical concern is what to do with the body. Although technological innovations continue apace, the most common options remain burial and cremation. According to a 2021 YouGov poll, people who identify as "practising religious" were more likely to prefer burial to cremation. In contrast, those who identify as non-religious, or as religious but not practising, expressed strong preference for cremation over burial.[1]

As a society, the UK has a high cremation rate. Of those who died in 1996, 71% were cremated[2], compared with 78% of those who died in 2019.[3] The findings of the 2021 poll support the statistic: 45% of Britons want to be cremated, while just 15% prefer burial.[4] One notable trend is the practice of direct cremation (also known as "simple", "unattended", or "basic cremation"), in which there is no formal funeral service; the body of the person who has died is cremated, and the ashes are available for collection later.[5] Due to restraints on funerals during the pandemic, the proportion of deaths followed by direct cremation rose to 18% in 2021.[6] It is likely that the trend will continue, as direct cremation offers relative affordability, flexibility of timing, and the assertion of greater control over post-death proceedings – including memorialisation activities.[7]

Memorialisation refers to the way in which memories about a person are laid down and recalled following their death.[8] One prominent strand of thinking emphasises the meaning-making dimensions of memorialisation that help the living to cope with grief.[9] Other studies cite the therapeutic function of memorialisation, particularly in collective acts and practices. The authors of a 2016 study argue that funerals help the bereaved to confront death, by celebrating the life of the deceased individual through the spoken eulogy, and by bringing mourners together to physically embody that person's diverse relationships.[10]

Memorialisation refers to the way in which memories about a person are laid down and recalled following their death.

In the UK, the face of memorialisation is changing. Until the late-20th century, religious funerals (particularly Christian) were the dominant choice.[11] Statisticians report a sharp decline in Christian funerals from 1999 to 2019; the Church of England observed a 50% decline over the same period, with other Christian denominations echoing a similar pattern.[12] According to a 2019 report by Co-op Funeralcare, Britain's largest funeral provider, just one in ten people now want a religious funeral.[13] Today, most funerals are taken by independent civil celebrants – a trend that looks likely to continue as demand for religious services declines.[14] Yet, celebrant-led funerals are not necessarily secular; at the request of the organiser, many incorporate spiritual or explicitly religious elements.[15]

Traditional memorialisation practices continue to be popular in the UK, but they co-exist alongside more personalised forms, such as memorial benches and trees, "ghost bikes" left at the site where a cyclist has been killed, and memorialisation tattooing – sometimes incorporating the ashes of the person who has died.[16] Indeed, with cremation on the rise, the British public is finding increasingly novel ways of commemoration through dispersing or preserving the ashes of their loved ones.[17]

3.2 Data analysis

Our research revealed divergent opinions regarding what people want physically, post-death, and a range of insights about the materiality of the body. For example, one Death Café focus group participant shared his anxiety about annihilation, describing death itself as a "void": "There's still a part of me which is really not comfortable with the idea of nothingness." In contrast, an end-of-life doula observed that her largely secular clients tend to express a sense of peace: "Most of the people I've worked with feel very connected to nature, and feel that they're part of nature, and that they will return." Running alongside this spectrum are a range of established religious beliefs, explored below.

The increasing popularity of cremation is driven partly by cost, and partly by a public perception that burials are more difficult to arrange.

Cremation

In line with the existing polling data, relevant death industry professionals described the increasing popularity of cremation – driven partly by cost, and partly by a public perception that burials are more difficult to arrange. Interviewees reported an increase in the number of requests for direct cremation in recent years, even before the pandemic.

The production of ashes through cremation gives rise to additional considerations and a broad spectrum of practice. While "no-witness scatterings" (i.e., in the absence of identifiable mourners or next of kin) may be the default for many deaths, cremation offers scope for additional personalisation, through choices made regarding

The production of ashes through cremation gives rise to additional considerations and a broad spectrum of practice.

what to do with the ashes. Interviewees described diverse possibilities:

— Jewellery created from ashes

— Community projects, such as the "People's Pyramid" in Toxteth, Liverpool[18]

— Storing the ashes at home

— Scattering the ashes in a place of meaning to the person who has died

— Scattering the ashes in a place of meaning to the person's loved ones

The practice of ash-scattering provoked lively debate amongst participants of one Death Café focus group, who debated the ethical implications of bespoke requests: "If you want to be in an ash pot, then keep it on the mantelpiece. But don't go tipping whoever it is over places where other people are going to be."

One funeral director commented on the ambivalence that people may feel about ash dispersal. He described clients who are reluctant to collect the ashes of their loved one from his office:

> *People tend not to dispose of ashes for quite a long time. I was forever trying to get people to collect ashes... It's bizarre that people don't want to pick up the ashes. But of course, that is the final part of the process.* (Funeral director)

Burials, particularly for the deaths of younger people, offer "a more substantial sense of place".

Burial

Despite the popularity of cremation, burials are still common practice. One Christian chaplain noted that burials, particularly for the deaths of younger people, offer "a more substantial sense of place". This sentiment was echoed by some participants of the Death Café focus group: "The idea of having my body lasting there and my bones in the ground for many centuries... is reassuring."

At times, the theological imperatives of certain religious practices can lead to tensions with secular professionals.

For some religious traditions, such as Islam and Judaism, burial is a vital theological practice. Interviewees from these traditions (including faith leaders, celebrants, and ritualists) emphasised the importance of a good burial, as evidenced in robust ritualistic frameworks (e.g., washing, shrouding, etc.) for the body of a person who has died. At times, the theological imperatives of certain religious practices can lead to tensions with secular professionals. One imam described his frustrations when arranging Muslim burials in non-Muslim graveyards – particularly with regard to the rapid timescale in which a person must be buried. From another perspective, a cemetery manager and former gravedigger expressed his own frustrations with this scenario; he described the challenges of responding to burial timeframes that may be unmanageable. Both interviewees pointed to the need for education and direct conversation.

The research also highlighted a notable trend regarding attitudes towards the repatriation of remains. One imam described how his grandparents' generation had desired their bodies to be returned to their homeland for burial, despite the theological complexities related to chemical preservation. For subsequent generations, however, repatriation has become less of a priority:

As a community [we] have realised, we are staying here for longer, and this is our home. If you look from the Islamic law point of view, perhaps it's better to stay here, because you're not getting pumped in with chemicals which may have alcohol. (Muslim faith leader)

This trend also resonates for Sikh communities, with one interviewee describing changing attitudes she has observed in her lifetime:

But now we're doing it [dispersing ashes] in flowing water where we've been given permission to do so, because there are certain people who have said: I do not want to be taken back to India. Some people will definitely say: "My father, grandfather-in-law, and grandmother-in-law (sic) specified: Do not want to go to India. Do not want to be taken to India for my ashes to be dispersed". And they did it at the River Trent. (Sikh academic)

Unasked questions: what do people need to know?

Death industry professionals lamented the paucity of public knowledge about biological processes like decomposition, and about the professional mechanics involved with retrieving and disposing a body. One cemetery manager and former gravedigger described the range of questions he is asked about cremation – for example, assumptions that it is common practice to "re-use" a coffin, or that a crematorium might incinerate multiple bodies simultaneously to save costs. Another death industry professional described people's surprise on learning the environmental impact of standard cremation – a fuel-intensive process that unleashes atmospheric pollutants. She wonders if growing environmental awareness might contribute to a trend towards "green burial".

Due to lack of information and the broader invisibility of death in society, people currently tend not to consider how they want others to engage with their body. Would they want an open-casket funeral, or loved ones involved with the washing and dressing process? One end-of-life doula advocates that families spend time with their dead: "That's something to be encouraged... because most people go through their entire lives without seeing a dead body. It's not surprising that there's so much fear and mystery."

Memorial services

Trends

We interviewed a range of people involved with organising and participating in memorial services, including celebrants, funeral directors, faith leaders, ritualists, and professional musicians. Collectively, they confirmed the trend towards increasing flexibility – due, in part, to the rise in direct cremation, and its separation of memorialisation practices from the burial or cremation of the body. Traditional funerals are giving way to "celebrations of life" that may incorporate a broader "spiritual spectrum". For example, one funeral

Traditional funerals are giving way to "celebrations of life" that may incorporate a broader "spiritual spectrum".

director described playing birdsong at the beginning of the ceremony, or "praying to Mother Earth, praying to the stars, or the moon, or power". Services that once would have been Christian by default are increasingly led by secular celebrants rather than by clergy.

The services themselves are increasingly personalised, with "less prescribed content" than in times past (charity leader and faith representative). One funeral director noted "more of an openness to move past Victorian traditions", citing as examples the decline of black mourning clothing and top hats. Another interviewee observed:

> It's much more likely now for people to feel able to wear yellow or have party poppers or everyone in the congregation gets a bar of chocolate. (Death industry professional)

Personal preferences are also expressed through choice of music. A long-serving Anglican priest, with expertise in liturgical music, described the rising popularity of secular songs such as "Somewhere over the rainbow" and "My way" by Frank Sinatra. Both songs featured in the top 20 most popular songs at a funeral in 2022.[19] The interviewee also noted that music is increasingly played or performed, rather than sung in community – a trend which the pandemic may have reinforced.

Another notable trend relates to personalised eulogies. Interviewees, across a broad spectrum of faith and spirituality, described how tributes to the person who has died now feature commonly in funerals and memorial services, in a way they did not a generation ago.

The impact of COVID-19

The pandemic continues to exert a profound influence on memorial events; interviewees (all interviewed between June and November 2022) were eager to reflect on the ongoing implications for their working practices. Funeral directors described bottlenecks at key stages of service provision, and the toll this takes on members of staff, particularly those at smaller businesses. One cemetery manager offered this example: During the pandemic, his cemetery temporarily ceased "no-witness ash scatterings (i.e., for people with no identifiable mourners or next of kin). This has resulted in a backlog that he now struggles to address, alongside the steady stream of incoming, post-pandemic work.

The rapid uptake of online streaming has facilitated participation in new ways.

Some interviewees identified positive outcomes of the pandemic, particularly for memorial services. One funeral director noted that restrictions on the number of attendees per funeral sometimes created powerful experiences of intimacy for mourners. Moreover, the rapid uptake of online streaming has facilitated participation in new ways – for example, by enabling a family member serving a prison sentence to "attend" a funeral, or widening the reach of those who can take part in Muslim funeral prayers. The elderly person focus group also appreciated how the online streaming of funerals allowed them to take part in services they otherwise would not have been able to attend. Not surprisingly, several interviewees expressed hope that this trend will continue.

Legacy and memorialisation

Alongside discussion of practices in the immediate aftermath of death, interviewees described longer-term practices relating to memorialisation. According to Catholic participants, Catholics pray for the souls of the departed in Purgatory (in Roman Catholic doctrine, the interim stage of purification before entering heaven), as well as offering Mass for the departed one month after their death. In Islam, a theological framework of "perpetual charity" leads to reward in the afterlife. Muslim participants described prayers recited to benefit the soul in the hereafter, alongside practices of charitable donation (e.g., to build wells or to support one's local mosque). According to one Glasgow-based imam, organ donation is increasingly recognised as a form of perpetual charity in which the donor will continue to be rewarded, even after death.

Practices of legacy were also discussed as forms of memorialisation. Although the topic of will-writing surfaced infrequently in discussion, those who raised it recognised its importance – even if they had yet to write one themselves. Death-preparation organisations like Kwaetus offer free guidance on writing wills, out of recognition that "when we are dead, others we love will live on".[20] In a similar focus on the future, the theme of organ donation emerged as a shared commitment amongst young people taking part in a university-based focus group. One participant described being inspired by the knowledge that her father had also registered as an organ donor.

1   "YouGov Death Study: Britons on their funeral and how long
    they think they will be remembered for", 6 October 2021, www.
    yougov.co.uk/topics/society/articles-reports/2021/10/06/
    yougov-death-study-britons-their-funeral-and-how-l

2   "International Statistics 1996", *The Cremation Society*, www.cremation.org.uk/
    international-statistics-1996

3   "International Statistics 2019", *The Cremation Society*, www.cremation.org.uk/
    International-cremation-statistics-2019

4   "YouGov Death Study", www.yougov.co.uk/topics/society/articles-reports/
    2021/10/06/yougov-death-study-britons-their-funeral-and-how-l

5   It should be noted that there is no sector-wide definition of "direct
    cremation". Kate Woodthorpe et al., "'My Memories of the Time We Had
    Together Are More Important': Direct Cremation and the Privatisation of
    UK Funerals", *Sociology* 56 3, pp. 556-573, https://journals.sagepub.com/
    doi/10.1177/00380385211036350

6   "Cost of Dying 2023 Report, *Sunlife*, https://www.sunlife.co.uk/funeral-costs/;
    "The Cost of Dying 2021 Report", Sunlife, www.sunlife.co.uk/siteassets/
    documents/cost-of-dying/cost-of-dying-report-2021.pdf/, p. 18.

7   "Funeral Costs in the UK, *Sunlife*, https://www.sunlife.co.uk/funeral-
    costs/#funeral-costs-in-the-uk
    Kate Woodthorpe et al., "My Memories of the Time We Had
    Together Are More Important", www.journals.sagepub.com/
    doi/10.1177/00380385211036350

8   "Remember Me. The Changing Face of Memorialisation." University of Hull,
    www.remembermeproject.wordpress.com/

9   "Remember Me. The Changing Face of Memorialisation." University of
    Hull, www.remembermeproject.wordpress.com/; Margaret Holloway et al.,
    "Spirituality in Contemporary Funerals", *Arts and Humanities Research Council
    and University of Hull* (2010), www.deathandsociety.org/uploaded-docs/ASDS-
    event-Hull%20Spirituality%20Report.pdf

10 Tara Bailey and Tony Walter, "Funerals against death", *Mortality* 21 2 (2016),
    pp. 149-166.

11 Clive Field, *Counting Religion in Britain*: 1970-2020: Secularization in Statistical
    Context (Oxford: Oxford University Press, 2022), p. 113.

12 Peter Brierley, *UK Church Statistics No 4: 2021 Edition* (Tonbridge: ADBC
    Publishers, 2020), p. 32; "Statistics for Mission 2019", *Church of England*, www.
    churchofengland.org/sites/default/files/2020-10/2019StatisticsForMission.
    pdf, p. 15; Clive Field, Counting Religion in Britain, p. 119.
    "Statistics for Mission 2019", www.churchofengland.org/sites/default/

files/2020-10/2019StatisticsForMission.pdf, p. 15.
Clive Field, Counting Religion in Britain, p. 119.

13 "Traditional funeral laid to rest", *Co-op*, 29 August 2019, www.co-operative.
coop/media/news-releases/traditional-funeral-laid-to-rest

14 "Funerals: 29th November-1st December 2016, *YouGov*, www.humanists.uk/
wp-content/uploads/Results-for-RELEASE-Funerals-OMNI_509-01.12.16.xlsx
Also see: Clive Field, Counting Religion in Britain, p. 121.

15 Sara Cox, "Funeral study challenges death of religion narrative", *Goldsmiths
University of London,* 19 January 2019, www.gold.ac.uk/news/religious-
resources-in-secular-funerals-/
Alan Stanley, "Open up to Christians taking civil funerals", *Church Times*, 26
February 2016, https://www.churchtimes.co.uk/articles/2016/26-february/
comment/opinion/open-up-to-christians-taking-civil-funerals; Margaret
Holloway et al., "'Funerals aren't nice but it couldn't have been nicer'. The
makings of a good funeral", *Mortality* 18 1 (2013), pp. 30-53.

16 "Displaying Self: Memorialisation in Contemporary Society", *Remember Me. The
Changing Face of Memorialisation*, www.remembermeproject.wordpress.com/
project-reports/
Ibid.

17 "Burying Traditions. The Changing Face of UK Funerals", Co-op Funeralcare,
2019, p. 20.

18 www.mumufication.com/about/

19 "20 popular funeral songs in 2022", *Funeral Guide*, www.funeralguide.co.uk/
blog/top-funeral-songs

20 www.kwaetus.com/

4. Afterlife

This chapter identifies, based on existing polling data and our interview data, current beliefs and understandings of the afterlife. In particular, it highlights different theologies surrounding the afterlife through both religious and non-religious frameworks, as well as differing concepts of the soul.

4.1 Polling analysis

Beliefs about the afterlife

It is important to acknowledge upfront that there is a limited amount of polling data on attitudes towards the afterlife. Polling that did exist reflected contradictory results, hence, it is necessary to treat them as indicative rather than definitive.

According to a longitudinal study from 1939 to 2008, Britons who believed in life after death stayed relatively consistent, around 40-50%.[1] The International Social Survey Programme (ISSP) came to a similar conclusion; its religion modules survey, comparing belief in life after death, stood at 48% in 1991 and at 43% in 2018.[2] Those not believing in life after death rose from 20% to around 40%, while the "don't know" category reduced from 20-30% to 5-15%.[3] Increasingly, people are deciding one way or another. However, while more people are choosing not to believe in an afterlife, this is still less than the relatively constant basis of those who do – in this study, at least.

According to a longitudinal study analysing the period from 1968 to 2008, a steady rate of 50-60% of people believed in heaven, with 30-40% saying "no" and the remaining "don't know".[4] On whether they believed in hell, however, those answering "no" steadily declined, while those answering "yes" to believing in hell marginally increased.[5] Conversely, according to the ISSP's religion modules survey comparing 1991 to 2018, the proportion expressing belief in heaven fell over the period (from 48% to 38%). Belief in hell, which was much lower in relative terms in 1991, stayed about the same.[6]

Current trends

Do the conclusions from these longitudinal studies still apply today? The picture is mixed. According to a study in 2021 on opinions on life after death in Britain, 51% of respondents believe they will continue to exist in some form after death, with 49% believing the opposite.[7] Along similar lines, 46% thought that people who have died could be aware of what is taking place in our lives, with 54% believing they could not.[8] These statistics suggest a fairly even match between those who believe in an afterlife and those who do not, weighted slightly towards the latter.

Conversely, according to a YouGov poll in 2021, a third of UK adults (33%) believe in an afterlife, but 42% do not. Three in ten Britons (30%) believe that heaven exists, with 18% saying they think hell exists too. Over half of the population (54%) don't believe in either. Similar conclusions were found in Theos' own poll through YouGov, indicating only 29% of UK adults believed that there was life after death.[9]

Amongst the non-religious, a fifth (20%) stated they definitely/probably believe in life after death.

Amongst the non-religious – the fastest growing group in the UK, with 52% of Britons now identifying as non-religious[10] – a 2022 Theos report found that a fifth (20%) stated they definitely/probably believe in life after death, and 27% of the non-religious believe in ghosts but only

11% believe in heaven.[11] The report found that while one in five believe in life after death, it was not in a traditionally Judeo-Christian religious sense, but rather embracing more readily aspects of New Age spirituality.

4.2 Data analysis

Frameworks of belief

Individuals interviewed for our research study embraced a wide range of religious and spiritual beliefs. Not surprisingly, the data reflects this breadth of diversity. Muslim interviewees spoke at length about Islam's vibrant imagery of the afterlife, amplified by regular preaching on the topic. In contrast, Jewish participants noted that the afterlife tends not to be discussed; as one ritualist commented: "Death doesn't end life, because the world carries on". In an interfaith focus group discussion, one Sikh academic described the afterlife in relation to reincarnation, cycling through millions of forms to the highest, human form: "That's the one I should be using to end that cycle of trans-migration and unite with God". In the same interfaith discussion, another academic emphasised the range of traditions within Hinduism, while pointing towards a shared vocabulary around reincarnation, death, liberation, and freedom from suffering.

Amongst Christians, belief in the afterlife varied considerably. What does it mean, in the words of one faith leader and academic, to "preach resurrection and hope in the face of death?" One Anglican priest described "dissonance" not only within the wider tradition,

What does it mean, in the words of one faith leader and academic, to "preach resurrection and hope in the face of death?"

but within the internal beliefs held by her clergy colleagues. She noted that "cognitive dissonance" between their "heart knowledge as well as head knowledge" can lead some clergy to struggle to engage in discussions about the afterlife. Some elderly participants, part of a Christian community group, were happy enough to think of the afterlife as spending eternity in communion with God and in the presence of God's eternal love. Although they were not able to articulate that idea in depth, they were content not to know what the afterlife entailed until they were there. Interestingly, as Christians, they did not fear the afterlife but rather feared the process of getting to the afterlife. A Catholic hospice chaplain, working in a theologically diverse context, described his increasingly frequent experience of conversations about Purgatory. He notes that these conversations, with hospice colleagues and members of the public, increased significantly during the pandemic. This decidedly amorphous understanding of the afterlife from a Christian perspective suggests the need for increased Christian theological education and thinking on the subject and its communication to its believers.

> **The decidedly amorphous understanding of the afterlife from a Christian perspective suggests the need for increased Christian theological education and thinking on the subject and its communication to its believers.**

A similar breadth of belief was also found amongst people who did not subscribe to or identify with a named religious tradition. In London, two community organisers described their involvement in a recent "Day of the Dead" arts festival; they encountered "diverse personal spirituality" and a public eager to engage with the theme. Several respondents, particularly those in public-facing roles, commented on the prevalence of nature-based spirituality, for example:

Most of [my clients] would think of themselves as spiritual, in that they feel part of the world. They feel very connected to nature. They feel that they're part of nature, and that they will return. (Funeral celebrant)

For other people, concepts of the afterlife may be more amorphous, such as the idea that the person who died is "going to a better place". One military chaplain observed that this phrase can bring comfort, particularly to those mourning a person who has died unexpectedly or by violent means. Indeed, death industry professionals working with largely secular clients described strength of hope in the afterlife. According to one long-serving funeral organist with extensive experience of secular crematorium services:

People will say: "Oh, I'm not religious at all. I don't believe in God and all that". I would say that almost 100% of those people wanted to believe, or believed, that something happens after [death]. I can't think of anyone who actually got up there and said: "I believe death is the end".

His observation was confirmed by funeral directors interviewed for this study, including one who described a non-religious client looking in the world around her for "signs and portents" of the afterlife.

Concepts of the soul

Closely tied to these discussions of the afterlife are diverse concepts of the soul. Some of the interviewees offered clear teachings from their religious traditions. For example, interviewees described the belief in Islam of the soul's painful

People who do not identify with a religious tradition may also hold onto spiritualities about the soul.

departure from the body; a Jewish metaphor of the body as a glove and the hand as its soul; and a Sikh belief that the crying of mourners prevents the soul from leaving the earth. Responses from Christian interviewees tended to be more diffuse, illustrating what one Anglican priest and liturgist described as a "collage of beliefs" and a "spiritual woodland". In her own ministry, she has encountered varied ideas about the soul – for example, through supporting people who have experienced visions of the dead; conducting rituals for her Caribbean parishioners as the soul of their loved one "passes over" gradually; and praying "with angels". Another Anglican priest emphasised links between the Christian tradition and "folk religion", citing the motif of "winged creatures" and a common experience of people "seeing" their loved ones as birds.

For those who do not adhere to a specific religion, there is no desire to say that death is the end.

People who do not identify with a religious tradition may also hold onto spiritualities about the soul. One funeral director, who works extensively with secular clients, described a common occurrence:

> *You're at the funeral and a butterfly lands on a grave, or a ray of sunshine erupts through a cloud. You will absolutely get people saying, 'He's here!' or, 'That's him!' You can just feel it, the way they look at each other.*

It is clear that beliefs about what happens after death are far from monolithic within faith traditions, while for those who do not adhere to a specific religion, there is no desire to say that death is the end. Instead, there is a rich variety of experiences in which people find meaning and signs of their loved ones' continued presence.

1 "Belief in life after death, Great Britain, all adults, 1939-2008", *British Religion in Numbers,* www.brin.ac.uk/wp-content/uploads/2016/06/Belief-After-Life-1939-2008.png

2 "Religious Change in Britain: Evidence from the 1991 and 2018 ISSP Religion Modules", *British Religion in Numbers,* www.brin.ac.uk/religious-change-in-britain-evidence-from-the-1991-and-2018-issp-religion-modules/

3 "Belief in life after death, Great Britain, all adults, 1939-2008", *British Religion in Numbers,* www.brin.ac.uk/wp-content/uploads/2016/06/Belief-After-Life-1939-2008.png

4 "Belief in heaven, 1968-2008", *British Religion in Numbers,* www.brin.ac.uk/wp-content/uploads/2016/06/Belief-in-heaven-1968-2008.png

5 "Belief in hell, 1968-2009", *British Religion in Numbers,* www.brin.ac.uk/wp-content/uploads/2016/06/Belief-in-hell-1968-2009.png

6 "Religious Change in Britain: Evidence from the 1991 and 2018 ISSP Religion Modules", *British Religion in Numbers,* www.brin.ac.uk/religious-change-in-britain-evidence-from-the-1991-and-2018-issp-religion-modules/

7 "British Opinions on Life After Death", Maru Public Opinion, 2021, www.marugroup.net/public-opinion-polls/uk/british-opinions-life-after-death

8 Ibid.

9 "YouGov Survey Results", Theos, 2020, https://docs.cdn.yougov.com/o93kio300s/YG-Archive-11082020-TheosSpirituality.pdf

10 "Religion: Identity, behaviour and belief over two decades", *British Social Attitudes,* www.bsa.natcen.ac.uk/media/39293/1_bsa36_religion.pdf

11 Hannah Waite, "The Nones: Who are they and what do they believe?", *Theos, 2022,* www.theosthinktank.co.uk/the-nones-who-are-they-and-what-do-they-believe

5. ... And the role of churches and faith communities?

Having outlined trends in the UK on dying, death, and the afterlife – from religious and non-religious perspectives – based upon existing polling data and interviewing experts and informed individuals, our report now explicitly turns to the role of churches and faith communities.

66

Churches and faith communities have an important role to play as pastoral carers and theological accompaniers.

We suggest that churches and faith communities have an important role to play as pastoral carers and theological accompaniers. We define "pastoral care" as a framework of emotional, social, and – crucially – spiritual support to those facing death and to the bereaved. We define "theological accompaniment" as a framework of walking alongside the dying and bereaved, through offering space and opportunity to explore distinctly religious understandings of living in the context of dying, death, and afterlife.

Most people will rely on family and friendship networks to support them through a dying or bereavement process. Pastorally, however, churches and faith communities offer a potential additional space for support and care when death approaches. Theologically, churches and faith communities help us prepare for death by encouraging wider conversation about the meaning of life and death, helping people explore themes of hope and continued existence after physical death.

Our report responds directly to a vision of how death and dying could be better navigated, in response to recent findings of *The Lancet Commission on the Value of Death* in January 2022. The Commission called for a "rebalancing"of society's approach to death.[1] One of its five principles states that "dying [should be] understood to be a relational and spiritual process rather than simply a physiological event."

Drawing on examples from our interview data, this section of the report outlines our main argument – that churches and faith communities bring pastoral care and theological accompaniment to the

Our report responds directly to recent findings of *The Lancet Commission on the Value of Death* which called for a "rebalancing" of society's approach to death.

dying, in the aftermath of death and in exploring the afterlife. At the same time, we suggest ways in which churches and faith communities could better fulfil their service of pastoral care and theological accompaniment.

Pastoral care and theological accompaniment to the dying

For many people, churches and faith communities offer pastoral care and theological accompaniment to the dying. Multiple chaplains whom we interviewed spoke of their role as one of "walking alongside" the dying. A Christian military chaplain understood his role as a

Multiple chaplains whom we interviewed spoke of their role as one of "walking alongside" the dying.

trusted friend, trusted companion, sometimes regarded as a subject matter expert, but sometimes you're just regarded as somebody who they feel will stand alongside them when they're going through the pain.

A Jewish chaplain working in a hospice articulated his role as one of "accompaniment", stating that a chaplain's purpose was to be a voice of reassurance and comfort for the dying person. During the COVID-19 pandemic, chaplains were among the few people still able to visit patients; they were still seen as vital to the healthcare profession to support and care for the dying. An imam and Muslim chaplain highlighted the distinctive role of chaplains compared to that of healthcare professionals. He stated:

As chaplains, our job is to support them [the dying person] from a spiritual, religious, pastoral perspective. A doctor's job obviously is different... [sic] more operational when it comes to dealing with death.

One Muslim chaplain commented that during the pandemic, it was a great responsibility but also a real privilege for the chaplain to often be the last person of faith the dying person saw.

While chaplains were recognised in their capacity to care pastorally for the dying, it was suggested that with more time and continued training, Christian clergy could better serve those dying in their community. A Christian representative spoke of the need for parish priests to know their communities better by being "in people's homes and in their kitchens talking to them" more than solely preaching in church. However, as someone working for the Church of England noted, there are concerns that parish priests did not have the time to accompany their parishioners on end-of-life matters due to an "overwhelming" workload. Furthermore, multiple interviewees suggested that clergy would benefit from continued training and experiencing death first hand – to "feel the rhythm" of death by working in a care home, experiencing the anxiety of people who are living with advanced dementia, witnessing upset families watching their loved ones wither away. Such suggestions, highlighted by a Christian representative, would make the clergy not only better at pastoral support but better people too.

This suggests that churches and other faith communities could or should use resources beyond clergy and chaplaincy. Some faith communities already provide pastoral support to the dying through informal support structures. A healthcare professional commented that they are crucial and should be regarded as being "just as important as the formal side of things". A good example of faith communities supporting the dying is the "End of Life Companions" programme run by The Art of Dying Well in partnership with the St Vincent de Paul Society (an international voluntary Catholic organisation). End of life companions are volunteers who, after training, serve those dying within *and outside* of their community, offering them pastoral and spiritual support according to the values of St Vincent de Paul. To date, 250 people have been trained to become an end of life companion.

Furthermore, churches and faith communities offer theological accompaniment to the dying through prayer. "Prayers for the dying" was one of the most visited pages on The Art of Dying Well website, attracting nearly 200,000 unique visitors principally on mobile devices, indicating "that they are potentially praying those prayers, either verbally or in their heads, in the moment" (Charity leader). Multiple Muslim interviewees highlighted the importance of Muslim chaplains and communities reading the Qur'an while someone was dying because

> *at the time of death, when the soul is removed from the body,*
> *that is an extremely painful experience for the person who is*
> *suffering. So, one of the ways to alleviate the suffering is like*
> *reading the Qur'an, and so on and so forth.* (Muslim faith
> leader)

In Hinduism too, a Hindu academic spoke of prayer
assemblies and the singing of hymns at the home.

Many people might fear the idea of theological
accompaniment, for fear that a chaplain or volunteer could
aggressively steer towards one version of the afterlife.
In reality, this is far from the truth. In fact, our research
suggested that if anything, chaplains are likely to err on the
side of caution. A Jewish chaplain described fielding questions
about heaven and hell, judgement of a soul, or whether Jesus,
Mohammed, or Buddha are waiting next to God. He shared
how he tends to respond with "maybe" and by suggesting to
the dying person that "whatever you are waiting for, whatever
you want to happen, will happen. Whatever you're dreading,
won't happen". In this way, he claimed that such an approach
provided more reassurance to the dying rather than religious
facts. Similarly, an Anglican priest stressed that the end-of-life
stage is not the time to try to convince someone of a particular
belief system:

> *I don't think my job at someone's deathbed is to persuade them*
> *that something is true, because they don't believe it to be true.*
> *That's just not my job. My job is to assure them that, you know,*
> *whatever they believe is fine.*

The boundary between chaplains relaying theological
assurances and not overstepping the natural limitations posed
by chaplaincy etiquette is a thin line to walk. However, given
that our study has found that the idea of an afterlife provides

comfort to the dying and the bereaved by offering a spiritual framework for navigating life and death, perhaps such an approach needs to be revisited or explored further.

Alongside pastoral care and theological accompaniment, multiple interviewees suggested that churches and faith communities can play a greater practical role by informing and educating the public about dying. A good example of this is the deathbed etiquette cards developed by The Art of Dying Well, which present Catholic, Jewish, and Muslim rituals at the end of life.[2] But churches and faith communities could do more. An Anglican priest suggested that churches could encourage dialogue on the topic via hosting Death Cafés. Another Christian interviewee suggested that churches and faith communities could be better at providing more practical support on dying, such as encouraging people to write wills, set up Do Not Resuscitate orders, and writing letters to loved ones. It was furthermore suggested that churches could incorporate references to death in Christian liturgy beyond Holy Week and Easter and within other sacraments – for example, during marriage preparation.

Churches and faith communities can play a greater practical role by informing and educating the public about dying.

Pastoral care and theological accompaniment in the aftermath of death

For many people in the UK, churches and faith communities play an important role in death and its aftermath – particularly in religious traditions and teachings, and through ritual frameworks for farewell. Alongside interviewees from Jewish, Muslim, Sikh, and Hindu backgrounds, we spoke at length to participants from Christian backgrounds with regard to memorialisation and post-death pastoral care.

Interviewees confirmed the increasing popularity of "celebrations of life", often at the expense of funerals that might otherwise be conducted in Christian churches.

Interviewees confirmed the increasing popularity of "celebrations of life", often at the expense of funerals that might otherwise be conducted in Christian churches. More than one respondent referred to a perception that clergy are less flexible than their independent counterparts. In the words of one funeral director: "When it becomes your main source of income, I think you are probably more flexible and easier to work with." A professional organist observed that music can be a potential source of conflict between mourners and the religious venue hosting the service – for example, priests conducting Mass in certain Roman Catholic parishes.

In addition to the perception of greater flexibility, a secular venue may also offer freedom of expression:

> This is where crematoriums have the edge, because people don't feel by being in a church... You can swear, for example... People feel that they can't express themselves in that same way, in a church. (Funeral musician)

Church perceptions aside, there is also a sense in which "celebration" simply sounds more appealing than "funeral". One funeral director described a common practice amongst his colleagues, in which mourners opting for a "celebration of life" will automatically be directed to a secular celebrant.

Nonetheless, the interviews revealed that secular memorial services include considerable spiritual – and often explicitly Christian – content. The Lord's Prayer (traditional version) and Psalm 23 remain popular readings, even at otherwise secular celebrations. An Anglican priest and liturgist described the Lord's Prayer as a "cultural prayer as much as a religious prayer", noting that "most people will know it, even if they don't believe it". As one musician observed, "People want the best. They want the benefit of the religious element, but they wouldn't want that religiosity to take away from being able to speak about the person."

The interviews revealed that secular memorial services include considerable spiritual – and often explicitly Christian – content.

Even for non-believers, a Christian funeral may offer appealing iconography and aesthetics. One Death Café focus group participant, who identified as "non-religious", valued Christian imagery for its strong association with death and burial rituals. He wondered: "Would I want a ceremony, although I'm not baptised?" And contrary to the trends observed both in the polling data and in our research, one funeral director reported:

> We have had a number of people recently who said, "I'm not Christian, but I want to have my funeral in a church. Can you ask the vicar whether they can use bits from the Book of Common Prayer?"

Secular services offer flexibility for some mourners, but there may also be downsides. Multiple interviewees expressed professional and pastoral frustrations with crematoriums.

Critiques of crematorium operations and cultures included descriptions such as "conveyor belt" and "assembly line". Furthermore, a former gravedigger shared how financial incentives can lead some celebrants to engage in irresponsible scheduling. By way of example, he described working previously with a "greedy" individual:

> *He would take any job he could get. He would sometimes stitch us up. We'd have a 10am chapel [service]. If no one turns up by quarter past, he's at the grave. And he's rushing because he's got an 11am appointment in the crematorium.*

This interviewee also shared examples in which an over-committed celebrant would instruct him to start filling a grave without the family present – leading to conflict when the family did arrive on site.

66

Another potential drawback of celebrant-led services is the pressure for mourners to emphasise "celebration" at the expense of other emotions.

Another potential drawback of celebrant-led services is the pressure for mourners to emphasise "celebration" at the expense of other emotions. A London-based funeral director expressed frustration with a common media perception that "funerals are becoming less funeral and becoming more a celebration... I sometimes read in the paper that it's all kind of like champagne."

She emphasised that her experience of working with grieving families is more nuanced than the media headlines would suggest:

> *You can't impose a mood on a bereavement... It's not like the older you are, the less sad people will be... And there are other circumstances, when a teenager dies by suicide, where you can't*

say: "It's a celebration of life"... There should be space and time made for the sadness, or the rage, and also for the joy and the gratitude.

She noted a "growing awareness" amongst her largely secular clients of the importance of emotion and how it might be expressed within and through a memorial service.

Faith leaders interviewed for this study, across a spectrum of religions, emphasised the importance of bereavement support – through funerals that can accommodate the emotional complexities of death, through theological accompaniment, and through ongoing pastoral care. In contrast to a secular celebrant's time-limited engagement for a specific memorial event, in theory, a faith community offers ongoing pastoral contact leading into, through, and beyond the funeral.

I think there's something about somebody who then keeps connection with the family after the death, the ongoing pastoral care, so that people can talk about it and express their feelings and process. Process their loss; process their anger with God.
(Christian chaplain)

Interviewees spoke at length about the nature of bereavement and the too-short timescale that contemporary society tends to allocate for grieving: "You can't learn how to handle grief. You can learn how to cope" (Jewish ritualist); "We've lost things like recovery" (Anglican priest).

There is scope for churches and faith communities to (re)claim a role that offers meaningful ritual, community support, and space for grappling with the nuanced emotional complexities of death.

In the words of one Methodist military chaplain with extensive personal and professional experience of bereavement:

> *We are changed [by bereavement]. We need a theology that helps us to remain whole people in that, and still remain open to the needs of others, even in the midst of where we're at.*

Despite – or perhaps because of – increasing public appetite for secular "celebrations of life", there is scope for churches and faith communities to (re)claim a role that offers meaningful ritual, community support, and space for grappling with the nuanced emotional complexities of death.

"Those who have a sense of the spiritual...that sense that life doesn't end here, are very often less agitated, towards the end."

Pastoral care and theological accompaniment in exploring the afterlife

The idea of an afterlife (however defined) may offer comfort to a person contemplating their own death or mourning the death of a loved one. One Christian charity leader expressed anecdotally that "those who have a sense of the spiritual...that sense that life doesn't end here, are very often less agitated, towards the end."

For many others, however, sheer uncertainty about the unknown can be a source of great anxiety and fear. According to death industry professionals and faith leaders interviewed for our project, fear and anxiety are commonly experienced, regardless of religious affinity. When asked about the fears that people express, one end-of-life doula observed: "The number one theme would be that people are very anxious about what's going to happen to them after they die." She described three broad categories of anxiety: people who feel that they have not been "good at their religion"; people who hold no conception of the afterlife and are "really freaked out that death is just nothing"; and people who simply fear the unknown.

Emerging from this research is the current absence of discussion about the afterlife – within faith communities, between faith communities, and between faith traditions and wider society. An academic spoke of running research workshops with clergy and remarking:

Emerging from this research is the current absence of discussion about the afterlife.

> *There were very ambivalent relationships with the kind of orthodox Christian teaching on death and also the funeral liturgy... Some of them, actually, I don't think believed in the resurrection, other than the kind of metaphorical idea.*

To this end, we need to reflect at all scales of society, starting at the level of the individual. This is particularly relevant for those in roles of pastoral accompaniment and faith leadership. In the words of an Anglican academic and practitioner, it is important to wrestle with one's "hermeneutic circle":

> *You need to spend a good deal of time reflecting on the reality of your ministry and your experience, your own personal bereavement history, and your feelings about those [inherited] doctrines, in order to engage.*

It is worth noting that one psychologist, who conducts research on fears about death, expressed scepticism "that what you believe makes a difference to how you respond to death". He would like to see religious communities do more to encourage conversation about the afterlife. For people on the margins of religions, or outside it altogether, this may be the best service that communities of faith can offer. As one humanist funeral director observed:

"When I speak to my friends who have faith, the privilege they have is they have figured out that there is a part inside themselves that is beyond the day-to-day".

When I speak to my friends who have faith, the privilege they have is they have figured out that there is a part inside themselves that is beyond the day-to-day, and they know that that exists. They can draw on it, and they know how to feed it... It's a rocky path to build from scratch. The answer is not for everyone to quickly join religion. Faith leaders can play a role in helping people locate that place.

Her words emphasise a recognition that the teachings and accompaniment of the Christian faith can provide a spiritual framework for navigating life in all its complexities – including, implicitly, bereavement, the approach towards death, and what lies beyond.

1 Libby Sallnow et al., "Report of the Lancet Commission on the Value of Death: bringing death back into life", *The Lancet* (2022), pp. 837-884.

2 "Deathbed etiquette", *The Art of Dying Well*, https://www.artofdyingwell.org/ caring-for-the-dying/deathbed-etiquette/etiquette/

Conclusion

We began our research by asking what role churches and faith communities currently play, in the context of current trends on, and attitudes towards, dying, death, and the afterlife in the UK. We ended our report by reflecting on the extent to which churches and faith communities are – and could be better at – offering pastoral care for, and theological accompaniment to, the dying and the bereaved.

Traditionally, churches and faith communities have been the custodians of death in the UK. But is this still the case? And if so, for how long will it remain?

Further research is needed to explore the extent to which churches and faith communities remain the keepers of death, or whether secular alternatives have overtaken them. Our research has highlighted a mixed picture. For example, chaplains are still valued in their pastoral accompaniment of the dying, but secular end-of-life doulas are increasingly popular. The rise of "celebrations of life" now rival religious funerals, yet Christian vocabulary in the memorialisation of the dead is still desired by the non-religious. The communication of theologies of death and the afterlife appears to be sparse, yet there is an openness and willingness to explore the afterlife through spiritual frameworks to calm fears that arise from dying.

Are churches and faith communities still the keepers of death? Our research has highlighted a mixed picture.

In the context of this mixed picture, death industry professionals and wider society need to understand the continued significance of faith and religion. Churches and

The practice and lexicon of death is rooted in Christian rituals and language.

faith communities play an important role in accompanying the dying and the bereaved, both pastorally and theologically – just as they do at other key life stages, from womb to tomb, through joy and grief. The practice and lexicon of death is rooted in Christian rituals and language, which still offer a resource for religious and non-religious alike. Churches and faith communities bring an inherited wisdom and years of practice as the keepers of death – a role that cannot be ignored or downplayed.

Churches and faith communities have an opportunity to re-weave the relationship between religion and death.

However, are we on the cusp of change? Churches and faith communities have an opportunity to re-weave the relationship between religion and death. This vital task calls for increased conversation about dying, death, and the afterlife – within and between faith communities, between death industry professionals and faith leaders/communities, and amongst the non-religious. This new relationship between religion and death calls for better public education, and for faith communities to participate in disseminating information to wider society about the process of dying and death, including what happens to the physical remains of a person. Furthermore, it requires churches and faith communities to reflect on their vocation as pastoral carers and theological accompaniers; to strive to improve practices for the dying and the bereaved; and to better help people explore the meaning of life and death, and the themes of hope in the continued existence after physical death. Churches and faith communities have a timely opportunity to re-examine, to challenge, and to amplify their role.

Our report began by considering death as a topic that is increasingly spoken about in public yet rarely discussed personally. Death need not be shrouded in silence. Churches and faith communities have a real opportunity to re-weave the shroud. By (re)integrating the role of religion in death, they can facilitate more open, honest, and life-giving understandings of dying, death, and the afterlife. In achieving this, we can strive to become a society that can die well and, in turn, live well.

Recommendations

We make a limited set of recommendations to churches and faith communities, and to death industry professionals.

Recommendations to all death industry professionals:

— Facilitate increased conversations on death, dying, and the afterlife between death industry professionals and churches and faith communities, in order to increase understanding and to address tensions.

— Develop common ground between the non-religious and the explicitly religious, in order to facilitate healthy conversations about death, dying, and the afterlife.

— Share understandings and best practice within and between faith communities, on death, dying, and the afterlife.

— Develop learning resources to educate the public about the dying process.

— Develop learning resources to educate the public about death and its aftermath: biological, procedural, etc.

— Familiarise the public with the reality of death (e.g. through the arts as a creative channel or through devising a "death curriculum" for children).

Recommendations specific to churches and faith communities:

— Improve communication of theological beliefs about the afterlife.

— Improve communication regarding the theological significance of religious funerals.

— Develop and improve training on death and bereavement, to ensure "best practice" pastoral care and theological accompaniment to the dying and the bereaved.

— Facilitate and increase practical, public engagement through hosting Death Cafés, will writing workshops, and bereavement support groups.

Theos – enriching conversations

Theos exists to enrich the conversation about the role of faith in society.

Religion and faith have become key public issues in this century, nationally and globally. As our society grows more religiously diverse, we must grapple with religion as a significant force in public life. All too often, though, opinions in this area are reactionary or ill informed.

We exist to change this

We want to help people move beyond common misconceptions about faith and religion, behind the headlines and beneath the surface. Our rigorous approach gives us the ability to express informed views with confidence and clarity.

As the UK's leading religion and society think tank, we reach millions of people with our ideas. Through our reports, events and media commentary, we influence today's influencers and decision makers. According to *The Economist*, we're "an organisation that demands attention". We believe Christianity can contribute to the common good and that faith, given space in the public square, will help the UK to flourish.

Will you partner with us?

Theos receives no government, corporate or denominational funding. We rely on donations from individuals and organisations to continue our vital work. Please consider signing up as a Theos Friend or Associate or making a one off donation today.

Theos Friends and Students

— Stay up to date with our monthly newsletter

— Receive (free) printed copies of our reports

— Get free tickets to all our events

£75/ year
for Friends

£40/ year
for Students

Theos Associates

— Stay up to date with our monthly newsletter

— Receive (free) printed copies of our reports

— Get free tickets to all our events

— Get invites to private events with the Theos team and other Theos Associates

£375/ year

Sign up on our website:
www.theosthinktank.co.uk/about/support-us

Recent Theos publications include:

The Nones: Who are they and what do they believe?

Hannah Waite

A Torn Safety Net: How the cost of living crisis threatens its own last line of defence

Hannah Rich

'Science and Religion': Moving away from the shallow end

Nick Spencer and Hannah Waite

Valuing Women: Making women visible

Kathryn Hodges

Beyond Left and Right: Finding Consensus on Economic Inequality

Hannah Rich

Just Work: Humanising the Labour Market in a Changing World

Paul Bickley

Relationships, Presence and Hope: University Chaplaincy during the COVID–19 Pandemic

Simon Perfect

The Church and Social Cohesion: Connecting Communities and Serving People

Madeleine Pennington

Ashes to Ashes

Practices around death and dying are changing rapidly. In particular, as the UK becomes less traditionally religious, there are growing preferences for cremation over burial and a rise of "celebrations of life" over traditional funerals. However, there still exists a wide range of religious and spiritual beliefs surrounding death and the afterlife. At the same time, in the aftermath of the COVID-19 pandemic, conversations about death are becoming more normalised – yet there is no corresponding increase in "death preparedness" (the extent to which individuals discuss or plan for the end of life).

In light of this changing picture, Theos and the Susanna Wesley Foundation investigated current trends on, and attitudes towards, dying, death, and the afterlife in the UK, and explored the role of churches and faith communities. We found continued shared concerns around what makes a "good death", including no pain/suffering, being surrounded by family/at home, peace/ reconciliation, and preparedness, but a wide range of religious and spiritual beliefs desired in memorialisation practices and when contemplating the afterlife.

While the religious landscape is changing, churches and faith communities have an important role to play in offering both pastoral care and theological accompaniment to the dying and the bereaved. There is a challenge and an opportunity for churches and faith communities to (re)claim their role – to re-weave the relationship between religion and death.

Dr Marianne Rozario is Senior Researcher and Projects Lead at Theos. She has a PhD in International Relations exploring the notion of Catholic agency in international society through the University of Notre Dame Australia, and a MA(Hons) in International Relations from the University of St Andrews. She is a Lecturer at St Mary's University, London.

Dr Lia Dong Shimada is Senior Researcher at the Susanna Wesley Foundation and Associate Chaplain at the University of Roehampton. She has a PhD in Cultural Geography from University College London, and a MA in Theology and Religious Studies from King's College London. Lia is the editor of 'Mapping Faith: Theologies of Migration and Community' (Jessica Kingsley Publishers, 2020).

Front cover image: pixnio.com

ISBN: 978-1-8382559-5-4

9 781838 255954